easy
organic cooking

p

This is a Parragon Publishing Book
First Published in 2006

Parragon Publishing
Queen Street House
4 Queen Street
Bath BA1 1HE
United Kingdom

This edition designed by Fiona Roberts.

ISBN: 1-40547-081-X

Printed in China

NOTE
This book uses metric and imperial measurements. Follow the same units of measurement throughout; do not mix metric and imperial. All spoon measurements are level: teaspoons are assumed to be 5 ml and tablespoons are assumed to be 15 ml. Unless otherwise stated, milk is assumed to be full fat, eggs and individual vegetables such as potatoes are medium, and pepper is freshly ground black pepper.

The times given for each recipe are an approximate guide only because the preparation times may differ accordingly to the techniques used by different people and the cooking times may vary as a result of the type of oven and other equipment used.

Recipes using raw or very lightly cooked eggs should be avoided by infants, the elderly, pregnant women, convalescents and anyone suffering from an illness. Pregnant and breast-feeding women are advised to avoid eating peanuts and peanut products.

contents

choosing to eat organic

Nowadays, we are becoming much more conscious of the food we eat and how it is produced. "You are what you eat" has become a familiar phrase, and given that there is a direct relationship between what we eat and the state of our health, it is clear that a safe, healthy diet is a very important part of our wellbeing.

Yet the choices we have to make can sometimes be overwhelming. Never before has there been such a wide variety of foods available. How do we choose the healthiest foods? How can we ensure that they are safe?

Advances in science have brought many welcome benefits in terms of food supply and our increased understanding of nutrition. These advances, however, have brought increasing concerns about modern methods of food production.

Now we also have to consider the advantages, disadvantages, and ethics of genetically modified (GM) foods. While some experts hail these as the new way to ensure pest-resistant plants and more durable foods, others are concerned about the techniques used and the possible long-term effects on our health. GM technology is now banned in organic farming, even in the production of organic animal feed. Every possible care is taken to avoid cross-pollination in order to ensure that organic crops are not contaminated by GM crops in neighboring fields.

Even if we disregard fears about GM foods, the use of synthetic fertilizers, chemical pesticides, and food additives raises concerns for the consumer. In addition, some food additives have been linked with health problems such as asthma and heart disease, and have been associated with conditions such as allergic reactions, hyperactivity, nausea, palpitations, and mood swings. It is no wonder that people are turning to organic food as a healthy and safe alternative.

So what exactly is organic food? There is a popular misconception that it is something for so-called health food fanatics and not for ordinary food-lovers, but this is not true. Cooking with organic ingredients produces delicious and enticing

Wonderfully fresh, organic ingredients can be made even more special with the addition of delicious sauces and dressings.

choosing to eat organic

Inventive dishes like stuffed bell peppers make the most of organic ingredients and are great for entertaining.

dishes. An organic meal could, for example, consist of a succulent fillet steak accompanied by white bread and a bottle of full-bodied red wine. This might be followed by an indulgent chocolate-and-cream dessert. Children can enjoy a dinner of hamburgers, fries, and tomato ketchup, made completely from organic ingredients. You may be surprised to find recipes in this book for dishes ranging from roasts to pizzas, and from puddings to meringues.

Organic food is simply any food that has been produced in a farming system that avoids the use of artificial chemicals, pesticides, and other additives. Organic farmers produce their foods by developing a healthy, fertile soil. They avoid using weedkillers, preferring instead to control weeds by mechanical cultivation techniques and by hand. Instead of using artificial pesticides, organic farmers use nature's way of controlling pests. They introduce insects that kill the pests but do not harm the crops. They plant and protect trees and hedges, to provide habitats for natural predators such as beetles and spiders, which, in turn help to keep down pests. Many organic farmers have revived the practice of crop rotation, moving the location of a crop each year over a three-year cycle in order to discourage pests that are attracted to particular crops. Organic farmers also rear animals in a more humane way, without feeding them cocktails of drugs, hormones, and antibiotics. Animals are kept in natural, free-range conditions and fed a more natural diet, ensuring they are healthy and can move around freely. Organic fish farms rear fish in an environment free of the chemicals that pollute so many inland and offshore waters. The end result is natural, healthier produce.

Organic farming is also kind to the environment. It encourages a wider diversity of plants and wildlife such as birds and butterflies, and nurtures the soil. Crop standards laid down by the National Organic Program (NOP) state that "land will have no prohibited substances applied to it for at least three years before the

choosing to eat organic

harvest of an organic crop." It takes time for the land to recover and for artificial chemical levels to fall. Organic farming helps restore a natural balance to exhausted soil, and increases its fertility.

The organic industry worldwide is becoming more highly regulated. On October 21, 2002, the National Organic Program (NOP) was put in place by the United States Department of Agriculture (USDA). The USDA organic seal guarantees consumers that a product contains at least 95 percent organic ingredients. When you are buying organic products, look out for this seal because it is a sign of the highest organic standards.

The production of organic food has been focused on fruit and vegetables, dairy products, and meat, but one of the largest recent increases is the market for organic wheat, rice, corn, barley, and oats. Several of the giant food manufacturing conglomerates are launching organic lines for sale in the major supermarket chains.

Once you have decided to switch to organic food as a healthy and safe alternative, you may find that you become more interested in eating locally produced food, in season, rather than produce from far-flung destinations that has accumulated many "air miles" to reach your table. If you have a farmers' market near you then you have the opportunity to buy fresh, wholesome produce that has not had to travel long distances to reach you. The traders will be only too anxious to talk to you about their production methods so you can learn at first hand how organic these methods are. If you have a yard or other outside space, you could even "grow your own"—you will find that nothing is more satisfying to cook and eat than home-grown produce.

Eating seasonally means that you'll benefit from more fresh, tasty, and affordable food all year round. These baked apples make a delicious dessert in fall and winter.

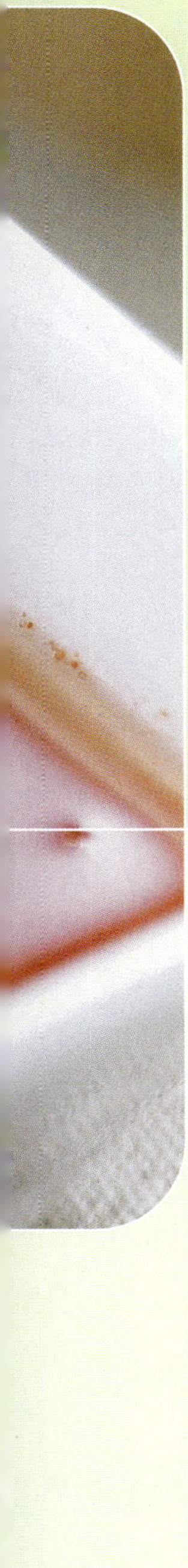

soups, appetizers and **salads**

There are some real treats in store for cooks and food lovers in the following pages. Many of the appetizers can double up as snacks or as satisfying meals in themselves. Add some fresh crusty bread to the Tomato & Bean Soup, for example, or the Ham & Lentil Soup, and you will find they make substantial lunches. The Stuffed Red Bell Peppers with Basil, and the Quick Mackerel Pâté are full of fresh flavor, while the salad recipes featured here are vibrant with color and texture. They make great accompaniments, appetizers, or light meals.

tomato & bean soup

SERVES 4 • PREP TIME 10 MINS • COOKING TIME 35 MINS

Heat the oil in a large pan over medium heat, add the onion, garlic, celery, and chili, and cook for 3 minutes, stirring occasionally.

Blend the tomato paste with the stock and add to the pan with the tomatoes. Bring to a boil, then reduce the heat and let simmer for 10 minutes.

Add the beans and salt and pepper to taste and let simmer for an additional 10 minutes.

Stir in the rice and cook for an additional 5 minutes, or until all the ingredients are piping hot. Serve sprinkled with the basil and with Parmesan cheese, if desired.

ORGANIC INGREDIENTS

1 tbsp olive oil

1 onion, chopped

2–3 garlic cloves, crushed

2 celery stalks, chopped

1 fresh red chili, seeded and chopped

1 tbsp tomato paste

4 cups vegetable stock

14 oz/400 g canned chopped tomatoes

7 oz/200 g canned red kidney beans, drained and rinsed

$10\frac{1}{2}$ oz/300 g canned cannellini beans, drained and rinsed

salt and pepper

generous $1\frac{1}{4}$ cups cooked brown rice

1–2 tbsp chopped fresh basil

freshly grated Parmesan cheese (optional), to serve

chunky vegetable soup

SERVES 4 • PREP TIME 10 MINS • COOKING TIME 40 MINS

Put the carrots, onion, garlic, potatoes, celery, mushrooms, tomatoes, and stock into a large pan. Stir in the bay leaf and herbs. Bring to a boil, then reduce the heat, cover, and let simmer for 25 minutes.

Add the corn and cabbage and return to a boil. Reduce the heat, cover, and let simmer for 5 minutes, or until the vegetables are tender. Remove and discard the bay leaf. Season to taste with pepper.

Ladle into warmed bowls and garnish with basil. Serve at once with crusty bread rolls.

ORGANIC INGREDIENTS

2 carrots, sliced

1 onion, diced

1 garlic clove, crushed

12 oz/350 g new potatoes, diced

2 celery stalks, sliced

4 oz/115 g closed-cup mushrooms, quartered

14 oz/400 g canned chopped tomatoes in tomato juice

2½ cups vegetable stock

1 bay leaf

1 tsp dried mixed herbs or 1 tbsp chopped fresh mixed herbs

½ cup corn kernels, frozen or canned, drained

2 oz/55 g green cabbage, shredded

freshly ground black pepper

few sprigs of fresh basil, to garnish (optional)

crusty whole-wheat or white bread rolls, to serve

chicken & broccoli soup

SERVES 4 – 6 • PREP TIME 10 MINS • COOKING TIME 35 MINS

Break the broccoli into small florets and cook in a pan of lightly salted boiling water for 3 minutes, drain, then plunge into cold water and set aside.

Melt the butter in a pan over medium heat, add the onion, rice, and chicken, and cook for 5 minutes, stirring frequently.

Remove the pan from the heat and stir in the flour. Return to the heat and cook for 2 minutes, stirring constantly. Stir in the milk and then the stock. Bring to a boil, stirring constantly, then reduce the heat and let simmer for 10 minutes.

Drain the broccoli and add to the pan with the corn and salt and pepper to taste. Let simmer for 5 minutes, or until the rice is tender, then serve.

ORGANIC INGREDIENTS

8 oz/225 g broccoli
salt and pepper
2 oz/55 g unsalted butter
1 onion, chopped
generous 1/8 cup basmati rice
8 oz/225 g skinless, boneless chicken breast, cut into thin slivers
scant $^1/_4$ cup all-purpose whole-wheat flour
$1^1/_4$ cups milk
2 cups chicken stock
generous $^1/_3$ cup corn kernels

ham & lentil soup

SERVES 4 • PREP TIME 20 MINS + 2 HRS TO SOAK • COOKING TIME 1 HR 30 MINS

Put the lentils into a large pan, pour over the stock and let soak for 2 hours. Add the garlic, onion, leek, carrot, tomatoes, and bay leaf, and season to taste with salt and pepper. Bring to a boil, then reduce the heat, cover the pan, and simmer for 1 hour, stirring occasionally.

Add all the potatoes with the ham, cover the pan again, and simmer for a further 25 minutes, or until the potatoes are tender.

Remove and discard the bay leaf. Transfer half the soup to a food processor and process for 1 minute, or until smooth. Return the mixture to the pan containing the rest of the soup, add the nutmeg, and adjust the seasoning to taste, then reheat gently until warmed through. Ladle into bowls, garnish with a spoonful of sour cream, and sprinkle over a little paprika. Serve with fresh crusty bread.

ORGANIC INGREDIENTS

- generous 1 cup red split lentils
- 6½ cups vegetable stock
- 1 garlic clove, chopped
- 1 onion, chopped
- 1 leek, chopped
- 1 large carrot, chopped
- 5 tomatoes, peeled and chopped
- 1 bay leaf
- salt and pepper
- 1 cup diced potatoes
- ½ cup diced sweet potato
- 1 cup diced smoked ham
- pinch of ground nutmeg

TO GARNISH

- 4 tbsp sour cream
- paprika
- crusty whole-wheat bread, to serve

stuffed red bell peppers with basil

SERVES 4 • PREP TIME 15 – 20 MINS • COOKING TIME 1 HR 15 MINS – 1 HR 30 MINS

Cook the rice in a pan of lightly salted boiling water for 20 minutes if using white rice, or 35 minutes if using brown. Drain, rinse under cold running water, then drain again.

Using a sharp knife, cut the tops off the peppers and reserve. Remove the seeds and white cores, then blanch the peppers and reserved tops in boiling water for 2 minutes. Remove from the heat and drain well. Heat half the oil in a large skillet, add the garlic and shallots, and cook, stirring, for 3 minutes. Add the celery, walnuts, tomatoes, lemon juice, and raisins and cook for a further 5 minutes. Remove from the heat and stir in the cheese, chopped basil, and seasoning.

Preheat the oven to 350°F/180°C. Stuff the peppers with the rice mixture and arrange them in a baking dish. Put the tops on the peppers, drizzle over the remaining oil, loosely cover with foil, and bake in the preheated oven for 45 minutes. Remove from the oven. Garnish with basil sprigs and serve with lemon wedges.

ORGANIC INGREDIENTS

¾ cup long-grain white or brown rice
4 large red bell peppers
2 tbsp olive oil
1 garlic clove, chopped
4 shallots, chopped
1 celery stick, chopped
3 tbsp chopped toasted walnuts
2 tomatoes, peeled and chopped
1 tbsp lemon juice
½ cup raisins
4 tbsp freshly grated Cheddar or soy cheese
2 tbsp chopped fresh basil
salt and pepper
sprigs of fresh basil, to garnish
lemon wedges, to serve

quick mackerel pâté

SERVES 4 • PREP TIME 25 MINS • COOKING TIME 0 MINS

Remove and discard any remaining bones from the mackerel fillets and put the fish into a small bowl. Mash the fish with a fork and combine with the yogurt, parsley, and lemon juice and rind. Season to taste with pepper.

Divide the pâté between 4 ramekins. Cover and let chill until required or serve at once.

To serve, garnish the pâté with lemon wedges and parsley sprigs and serve with the prepared vegetables and toasted whole-wheat bread.

ORGANIC INGREDIENTS

- **9 oz/250 g skinless smoked mackerel fillets**
- **generous 2/3 cup lowfat plain yogurt**
- **1 tbsp chopped fresh parsley**
- **1 tbsp lemon juice**
- **finely grated rind of 1/2 lemon**
- **freshly ground black pepper**
- **4 lemon wedges**
- **few sprigs of fresh parsley, to garnish**
- **1 red bell pepper, seeded and cut into chunky strips**
- **1 yellow bell pepper, seeded and cut into chunky strips**
- **2 carrots, cut into strips**
- **2 celery stalks, cut into strips**
- **slices whole-wheat bread, toasted and cut into triangles, to serve**

avocado salad with lime dressing

SERVES 4 • PREP TIME 20 MINS • COOKING TIME 0 MINS

Wash and drain the lettuce and arugula, if necessary. Shred all the leaves and arrange in the bottom of a large salad bowl. Add the scallions, tomatoes, and walnuts.

Halve, peel, and pit the avocados and cut into thin slices or small chunks. Brush with the lemon juice to prevent discoloration, then transfer to the salad bowl. Mix together gently.

Put the dressing ingredients into a screw-top jar, screw on the lid tightly, and shake well until thoroughly combined. Drizzle the dressing over the salad and serve immediately.

ORGANIC INGREDIENTS

2¼ oz/60 g mixed fresh red and green lettuce leaves

2¼ oz/60 g fresh arugula

4 scallions, finely diced

5 tomatoes, sliced

¼ cup chopped walnuts, toasted

2 avocados

1 tbsp lemon juice

LIME DRESSING

1 tbsp lime juice

1 tsp Dijon mustard

1 tbsp crème fraîche or sour cream

1 tbsp chopped fresh parsley or cilantro

3 tbsp extra-virgin olive oil

pinch of sugar

salt and pepper

feta cheese salad

SERVES 4 • PREP TIME 20 MINS • COOKING TIME 0 MINS

Wash and drain the salad leaves, if necessary. Shred the leaves and arrange in the bottom of a large salad bowl. Add the cilantro leaves, cucumber, scallions, tomatoes, and olives.

Cut the cheese into thin slices or small chunks, then transfer to the salad bowl. Mix together gently.

Put the dressing ingredients into a screw-top jar, screw on the lid tightly, and shake well until thoroughly combined. Drizzle the dressing over the salad and serve immediately.

ORGANIC INGREDIENTS

1¾ oz/50 g fresh green salad leaves

handful of fresh cilantro leaves

½ cucumber, chopped

4 scallions, finely diced

4 tomatoes, sliced

12 black olives, pitted and sliced

5 oz/140 g feta cheese (if organic feta cheese is unavailable, use organic goat cheese or mozzarella cheese instead)

CILANTRO DRESSING

4 tbsp extra-virgin olive oil

1 tbsp lime juice

1 tbsp chopped fresh cilantro

salt and pepper

smoked salmon & arugula salad

SERVES 4 • PREP TIME 20 MINS • COOKING TIME 0 MINS

Wash and drain the arugula, if necessary. Shred the leaves and arrange in 4 individual salad bowls or on 4 small plates. Top with the chopped parsley and scallions.

Halve, peel, and pit the avocados and cut into thin slices or small chunks. Brush with the lemon juice to prevent discoloration, then divide between the salad bowls. Mix together gently. Cut the smoked salmon into strips and scatter over the top.

Put the mayonnaise into a bowl, then add the lime juice and rind and the chopped parsley. Mix together well. Spoon some of the lime mayonnaise on top of each salad, garnish with parsley sprigs, and serve with lime wedges.

ORGANIC INGREDIENTS

1¾ oz/50 g fresh arugula

1 tbsp chopped fresh flat-leaf parsley

2 scallions, finely diced

2 large avocados

1 tbsp lemon juice

9 oz/250 g smoked salmon slices

LIME MAYONNAISE

½ cup mayonnaise

2 tbsp lime juice

finely grated rind of 1 lime

1 tbsp chopped fresh flat-leaf parsley

sprigs of fresh flat-leaf parsley, to garnish

lime wedges, to serve

three bean salad

SERVES 4 – 6 • PREP TIME 20 MINS • COOKING TIME 0 MINS

Arrange the salad greens in a salad bowl and set aside.

Thinly slice the onion, then cut in half to form half moons and put into a bowl.

Thinly slice the radishes, cut the tomatoes in half, and peel the beet if necessary and dice. Add to the onion with the remaining ingredients, except the nuts and cheese.

Put all the ingredients for the dressing into a screw-top jar and shake until blended. Pour over the bean mixture, toss lightly, then spoon on top of the salad greens.

Sprinkle over the nuts and cheese and serve at once.

ORGANIC INGREDIENTS

6 oz/175 g mixed salad greens such as spinach, arugula and frisée
1 red onion
3 oz/85 g radishes
6 oz/175 g cherry tomatoes
4 oz/115 g cooked beet
10 oz/280 g canned cannellini beans, drained and rinsed
7 oz/200 g canned red kidney beans, drained and rinsed
10½ oz/300 g canned flageolets, drained and rinsed
scant ⅓ cup dried cranberries
scant ½ cup roasted cashews
8 oz/225 g feta cheese, crumbled (if organic feta cheese is unavailable, use organic goat cheese or mozzarella cheese instead)

DRESSING

4 tbsp extra-virgin olive oil
1 tsp Dijon mustard
2 tbsp lemon juice
1 tbsp chopped fresh cilantro
salt and pepper

light meals and **side dishes**

The light meals in this section are deliciously satisfying, yet simple to make. The Red Onion Tartlets are delicious at any time of day, and excellent for picnics and lunchboxes. The succulent Salmon Morsels are quick and easy to prepare—ideal for those days when time is short—and the Baked Potatoes with Cream & Walnuts will have everyone clamoring for more. This chapter also features tempting side dishes, such as Steamed Vegetables en Papillotes and Classic Roast Potatoes, which make perfect accompaniments for a wide range of main courses.

baked potatoes with cream & walnuts

SERVES 4 • PREP TIME 15 MINS • COOKING TIME 1 HR 30 MINS

Preheat the oven to 375°F/190°C. Scrub the potatoes and pierce the skins several times with a fork. Place on a cookie sheet and cook in the preheated oven for 1¼ hours, or until cooked through. About 5 minutes before the end of the cooking time, melt 1½ tablespoons of the butter in a skillet over low heat, add the garlic and mushrooms, and cook, stirring, for 4 minutes, or until the mushrooms are tender. Remove from the heat and set aside.

Remove the potatoes from the oven and cut them in half lengthwise. Carefully scoop out the potato flesh into a bowl, leaving the skins intact. Add the remaining butter to the potato flesh, then stir in the herbs. Season to taste with salt and pepper. Spoon the mixture into the potato skins, then add a layer of mushrooms. Top with the cream, then the cheese. Return the potatoes to the oven and bake for another 10 minutes at the same temperature. Remove from the oven, scatter over the walnuts, and serve with a mixed salad.

ORGANIC INGREDIENTS

4 large baking potatoes
6 tbsp butter
1 large garlic clove, crushed
5½ oz/150 g mushrooms, sliced
1 tbsp snipped fresh chives
2 tbsp chopped fresh parsley
salt and pepper
¾ cup heavy cream
4 tbsp grated Cheddar or soy cheese
4 tbsp chopped lightly toasted walnuts, to garnish
fresh mixed salad, to serve

cheese & vegetable pockets

SERVES 4 • PREP TIME 20 MINS • COOKING TIME 50 MINS + 40 MINS TO CHILL

To make the pastry, sift the flour and salt into a large bowl. Rub in the butter until the mixture resembles bread crumbs. Add the water and mix to a dough. Cover with plastic wrap. Refrigerate for 40 minutes.

To make the filling, melt the butter in a large pan over low heat. Add the onion, potatoes, and carrots and cook, stirring, for 5 minutes. Add the green beans and water. Bring to a boil, reduce the heat, and simmer for 15 minutes. Remove from the heat, drain, rinse under cold running water, then drain again. Let cool.

Preheat the oven to 400°F/200°C. Cut the pastry into quarters and roll out on a floured work surface into 4 circles about 6 inches/15 cm in diameter. Mix the vegetables with the corn, parsley, cheese, and salt and pepper to taste. Spoon on to one half of each pastry circle. Brush the edges with water, then fold over and press together. Transfer to a greased baking sheet. Brush all over with milk. Bake in the preheated oven for 30 minutes until golden.

ORGANIC INGREDIENTS

PASTRY

1 3/4 cups whole-wheat flour, plus extra for dusting

pinch of salt

3 1/2 oz/100 g butter, diced, plus extra for greasing

4 tbsp cold water

2 tbsp milk, for glazing

FILLING

2 tbsp butter

1 onion, chopped

3/4 cup diced potatoes

3/4 cup diced carrots

1/3 cup chopped green beans

1/2 cup water

2 tbsp drained canned corn kernels

1 tbsp chopped fresh parsley

1/2 cup grated Cheddar or soy cheese

salt and pepper

cajun chicken salad

SERVES 4 • PREP TIME 20 MINS • COOKING TIME 20 MINS

Make 3 diagonal slashes across each chicken breast. Put the chicken into a shallow dish and sprinkle all over with the Cajun seasoning. Cover and let chill for at least 30 minutes.

When ready to cook, brush a stove-top grill pan with the corn oil, if using. Heat over high heat until very hot and a few drops of water sprinkled into the pan sizzle immediately. Add the chicken and cook for 7–8 minutes on each side, or until thoroughly cooked. If still slightly pink in the center, cook a little longer. Remove the chicken and set aside.

Add the mango slices to the pan and cook for 2 minutes on each side. Remove and set aside.

Meanwhile, arrange the salad greens in a salad bowl and sprinkle over the onion, beet, radishes, and walnut halves.

Put the walnut oil, mustard, lemon juice, and salt and pepper to taste in a screw-top jar and shake until well blended. Pour over the salad and sprinkle with the sesame seeds.

Arrange the mango and the salad on a serving plate and top with the chicken breast and a few of the salad greens.

ORGANIC INGREDIENTS

4 skinless, boneless chicken breasts, about 5 oz/140 g each

4 tsp Cajun seasoning

2 tsp corn oil (optional)

1 ripe mango, peeled, seeded, and cut into thick slices

7 oz/200 g mixed salad greens

1 red onion, halved and thinly sliced

6 oz/175 g cooked beet, diced

3 oz/85 g radishes, sliced

generous 3/8 cup walnut halves

2 tbsp sesame seeds

DRESSING

4 tbsp walnut oil

1–2 tsp Dijon mustard

1 tbsp lemon juice

salt and pepper

red onion tartlets

SERVES 4 • PREP TIME 35 MINS • COOKING TIME 40 MINS + 40 MINS TO CHILL

To make the pastry, sift the flour and salt into a bowl. Rub in the butter until the mixture resembles bread crumbs. Stir in the water, mix to a dough, then use your hands to shape the dough into a ball. Cover with plastic wrap and refrigerate for 40 minutes.

Meanwhile, melt the butter in a small skillet over low heat. Add the garlic and onions and cook, stirring, for 4–5 minutes until softened. Remove from the heat and let cool.

Preheat the oven to 350°F/180°C. Remove the dough from the refrigerator and roll out on a floured work surface. Using a 4-inch/10-cm round cookie cutter, cut out 12 circles and use them to line 12 greased, deep, fluted tartlet pans. Trim the pastry.

Put the egg, cream, and cheese into a bowl and whisk together. Add the onions and season with salt and pepper to taste. Divide the filling between the pastry cases, then bake in the preheated oven for 35 minutes until golden. Remove from the oven and serve hot or cold.

ORGANIC INGREDIENTS

PASTRY

7/8 cup all-purpose white or whole-wheat flour, plus extra for dusting

pinch of salt

6 tbsp butter, diced, plus extra for greasing

2 tbsp cold water

FILLING

1 tbsp butter

1 garlic clove, crushed

2 red onions, finely sliced

1 egg, beaten

1/2 cup heavy cream

1/2 cup freshly grated Parmesan or soy cheese

salt and pepper

salmon morsels

SERVES 4 • PREP TIME 15 MINS • COOKING TIME 15 MINS

Preheat the oven to 350°F/180°C. Using a sharp knife, cut the bread into thick slices. Drizzle with oil, transfer to an ovenproof dish, and bake in the preheated oven for 15 minutes.

Meanwhile, to make the topping, put the cream cheese into a bowl and add the chives and grated lemon rind. Mix together well.

Remove the bread slices from the oven and let cool. Spread a thick layer of the cream cheese mixture on one side of each bread slice, arrange strips of smoked salmon on the top, and serve with lemon wedges.

ORGANIC INGREDIENTS

2 crusty baguettes

3 tbsp olive oil

1 cup cream cheese

1 tbsp snipped fresh chives

1 tbsp finely grated lemon rind

3½ oz/100 g smoked salmon slices, cut into strips

lemon wedges, to serve

chicken wraps

SERVES 4 • PREP TIME 20 MINS • COOKING TIME 0 MINS

Combine the yogurt and mustard in a bowl and season to taste with pepper. Stir in the chicken and toss until thoroughly coated.

Put the lettuce, cucumber, celery, and grapes into a separate bowl and mix well.

Fold a tortilla in half and in half again to make a cone that is easy to hold. Half-fill the tortilla pocket with the salad mixture and top with some of the chicken mixture. Repeat with the remaining tortillas, salad, and chicken. Serve at once.

ORGANIC INGREDIENTS

generous 2/3 cup lowfat plain yogurt
1 tbsp whole-grain mustard
freshly ground black pepper
10 oz/280 g cooked skinless, boneless chicken breast, diced
5 oz/140 g iceberg lettuce, finely shredded
3 oz/85 g cucumber, thinly sliced
2 celery stalks, sliced
1/2 cup black seedless grapes, halved
8 x 8-inch/20-cm soft flour tortillas or 4 x 10-inch/25-cm soft flour tortillas

cheese & ham pizzas

SERVES 4 • PREP TIME 10 MINS • COOKING TIME 50 – 55 MINS + 40 MINS TO RISE/COOL

To make the bases, mix together the flour, yeast, and salt in a bowl. Make a well in the center and stir in the oil and enough of the water to make a smooth dough. Knead on a lightly floured work surface for 5 minutes. Wash the bowl and brush with oil. Shape the dough into a ball and return to the bowl. Cover with plastic wrap. Let rise for 30 minutes or until doubled in size. Knead the dough for another 2–3 minutes, return to the bowl, and cover again.

Meanwhile, heat the oil in a large skillet over medium heat and cook the garlic, stirring, for 3 minutes. Add the tomatoes and tomato paste and cook for 20–25 minutes, or until thickened. Let cool.

Preheat the oven to 400°F/200°C. Divide the dough into 4 pieces, shape into balls, then roll out into flat circles 1/2 inch/5 mm thick. Spread over the tomato sauce. Top with mozzarella, ham, and mushrooms. Add salt and pepper to taste, then drizzle with oil. Bake for 25 minutes and serve garnished with basil leaves.

ORGANIC INGREDIENTS

PIZZA BASES

- 2 2/3 cups all-purpose flour, plus extra for dusting
- 1 envelope (1/4 oz/7 g) active dry yeast
- 1 tsp salt
- 1 tbsp extra-virgin olive oil, plus extra for brushing
- 1 cup lukewarm water

TOPPING

- 1 tbsp olive oil, plus extra for drizzling
- 2 garlic cloves, crushed
- 1 lb 12 oz/800 g canned chopped plum tomatoes
- 1 tbsp tomato paste
- 9 1/2 oz/275 g mozzarella or soy cheese, diced
- 8 oz/225 g lean ham, cut into small pieces
- 4 1/2 oz/125 g mushrooms, sliced
- salt and pepper
- fresh basil leaves, to garnish

steamed vegetables en papillotes

SERVES 4 • PREP TIME 20 MINS • COOKING TIME 35 MINS

Preheat the oven to 400°F/200°C. Fill a large pan with water and bring to a boil. Blanch the potatoes, carrots, and parsnip in the boiling water for 2 minutes. Drain, rinse under cold running water, then drain again. Set aside.

Cut 4 squares of parchment paper, each measuring about 10 inches/ 25 cm across, and arrange in a roasting pan. Scrunch up the edges of each square a little to make them into shallow "bowls," then divide the blanched vegetables between them. Top with the sugar snap peas and season to taste with salt and pepper.

In a bowl, mix the garlic with the parsley, then stir in the wine. Pour the mixture over the vegetables. Bring the edges of the paper over the vegetables and close tightly to enclose the contents within the pockets. Transfer to the preheated oven and bake for 30 minutes, or until the vegetables are tender. Remove from the oven and serve in the pockets.

ORGANIC INGREDIENTS

1 lb/450 g small new potatoes, halved lengthwise
2 carrots, halved lengthwise and sliced
1 parsnip, cut into small pieces
1 cup sugar snap peas
salt and pepper
1 large garlic clove, crushed
2 tbsp chopped fresh parsley
1 cup white wine

stuffed tomatoes

SERVES 4 • PREP TIME 20 MINS • COOKING TIME 20 – 25 MINS + 1 HR TO SOAK/COOL

Put the bulgur wheat into a heatproof bowl and cover with the boiling water. Let soak for 1 hour, or until most of the water has been absorbed. Meanwhile, cut the red bell pepper halves in half again to give quarters. Arrange skin side up on a broiler rack and cook under a preheated medium–hot broiler for 10 minutes, or until the skins are evenly blackened. Remove from the broiler, place in a plastic bag, and set aside for 15 minutes. When cool enough to handle, remove and discard the skins. Chop the flesh.

Cut the tomatoes in half, scoop out the seeds and discard. Drain the wheat well and place in a large bowl. Add the scallions, parsley, cilantro, nuts, and red bell pepper. Season to taste with salt and pepper and mix well. Spoon the mixture into the tomato shells and transfer them to a broiler rack covered with foil. Drizzle over the oil and cook under a preheated medium–hot broiler for 10–15 minutes, or until the tomatoes are tender. Serve hot with a salad.

ORGANIC INGREDIENTS

1 cup bulgur wheat

2½ cups boiling water

1 red bell pepper, halved and seeded

4 beefsteak tomatoes

4 scallions, chopped

2 tbsp chopped fresh parsley

1 tbsp chopped fresh cilantro

¼ cup raw unsalted cashew nuts, halved and lightly toasted

salt and pepper

1 tbsp lemon-flavored oil or olive oil

salad, to serve

classic roast potatoes

SERVES 4 • PREP TIME 10 MINS • COOKING TIME 1 HR 30 MINS

Preheat the oven to 400°F/200°C. Using a sharp knife, cut the potatoes in half, or into quarters if very large, then arrange in a roasting pan. Sprinkle over the salt, then season to taste with pepper and paprika.

Pour the oil over the potatoes, then turn them in the oil until thoroughly coated. Transfer to the preheated oven and roast, basting occasionally, for $1\frac{1}{2}$ hours, or until golden brown and tender. Remove from the oven and serve at once.

To ring the changes, try adding 1 crushed garlic clove and 1 tablespoon of lemon juice to the oil before pouring over the potatoes. They will add a deliciously different flavor and the aroma will be irresistible.

ORGANIC INGREDIENTS

900 g/2 lb medium–large mealy potatoes, peeled

½ tsp salt

pepper

paprika

½ cup vegetable oil

main dishes

The recipes in this chapter are truly inspirational and mouthwatering. The Trout Fillets with Lime, Sesame & Chili and the Salmon Steaks with Lime Salsa will delight fish lovers everywhere, and the meat and poultry dishes will satisfy every taste. From Traditional Roast Chicken, or Maple Roast Lamb with Cider, to Stuffed Roast Pork with Garlic, each dish uses deliciously fresh and succulent ingredients. And the vegetarian dishes are hard to beat. You will find the Baked Vegetable Crumble and Mushroom Risotto every bit as exciting and satisfying as the meat dishes.

baked vegetable crumble

SERVES 4 • PREP TIME 25 MINS • COOKING TIME 1 HOUR

To make the filling, melt the butter in a large pan over low heat, add the garlic and leek, and cook, stirring, for 4 minutes until softened. Add the potatoes, carrots, parsnips, broccoli, and tomatoes and cook, stirring occasionally, for 12–15 minutes. Stir in the flour and cook for 1 minute. Remove from the heat and gradually stir in the milk and stock. Return to the heat and cook, stirring, until thickened. Add the herbs and seasoning. Simmer for 20 minutes.

Meanwhile, to make the crumble, put the flour into a large bowl, then rub in the butter until the mixture resembles bread crumbs. Add the cheese, walnuts, almonds, and thyme and mix well. Preheat the oven to 400°F/200°C.

Remove the vegetable mixture from the heat and transfer to an ovenproof dish. Spoon the crumble over the top and press down gently. Bake in the preheated oven for 25 minutes, or until golden and the vegetables are cooked through. Serve hot.

ORGANIC INGREDIENTS

VEGETABLE FILLING

3 tbsp butter
1 garlic clove, crushed
1 large leek, sliced
1/2 cup diced potatoes
3/4 cup diced carrots
3/4 cup diced parsnips
scant 1 cup small broccoli florets
3 tomatoes, cut into eighths
3 tbsp whole-wheat flour
1/2 cup lowfat milk
3/4 cup vegetable stock
1 tbsp chopped fresh parsley
1 tbsp chopped fresh thyme
salt and pepper

CRUMBLE TOPPING

3/4 cup whole-wheat flour
6 tbsp butter
3/4 cup grated Cheddar or soy cheese
1/4 cup finely chopped walnuts
1/3 cup ground almonds
1 tbsp chopped fresh thyme

vegetable pasta with tofu

SERVES 4 • PREP TIME 15 MINS • COOKING TIME 10 MINS

Bring two large pans of lightly salted water to a boil. Add the asparagus and peas to one pan and cook for 3 minutes. Drain, rinse under cold running water, then drain again. Put the pasta into the other pan and cook for 3–4 minutes, or until tender but still firm to the bite.

While the pasta is cooking, melt the butter in a large skillet over medium heat. Add the mushrooms and tofu and cook, stirring, for 2 minutes. Add the pine nuts, asparagus, and peas, then stir in the cream cheese and Cheddar or soy cheese and season to taste with salt and pepper. Cook for another 2 minutes.

Drain the pasta and divide among 4 serving plates. Remove the vegetable and tofu sauce from the heat and spoon it over the pasta. Scatter over the freshly grated Parmesan cheese. Garnish with basil sprigs and serve immediately.

ORGANIC INGREDIENTS

5½ oz/150 g baby asparagus spears, cut into 2-inch/5-cm lengths
1 cup shelled peas
8 oz/225 g fresh tagliatelle or spaghetti
2 tbsp butter
5½ oz/150 g mushrooms, sliced
7 oz/200 g tofu (drained weight), cut into small chunks
½ cup pine nuts, toasted
¾ cup full-fat cream cheese
¾ cup grated Cheddar or soy cheese
salt and pepper
4 tbsp freshly grated Parmesan cheese
sprigs of fresh basil, to garnish

mushroom risotto

SERVES 4 • PREP TIME 15 MINS • COOKING TIME 30 – 35 MINS

Heat the oil in a large skillet over low heat, add the garlic and mushrooms, and cook, stirring, for 3 minutes. Remove from the heat and set aside.

Heat the butter in a large pan over medium heat, add the shallots, and cook, stirring, for 3 minutes. Add the rice and cook, stirring constantly, for 2 minutes, then pour in the wine and lemon juice and stir until the liquid is almost absorbed. Add a ladleful of the simmering stock, and cook, stirring, until it is absorbed. Keep adding the stock, a ladleful at a time, waiting for each ladleful to be absorbed before adding the next.

When almost all the liquid has been absorbed, stir in the mushrooms, lemon rind, and salt and pepper to taste. Continue to cook, stirring, until the liquid has been completely absorbed, then remove from the heat and stir in the parsley and cilantro. Serve immediately, garnished with parsley or cilantro sprigs.

ORGANIC INGREDIENTS

3 tbsp olive oil
2 large garlic cloves, crushed
14 oz/400 g mushrooms, sliced
3 tbsp butter
4 shallots, chopped
1½ cups risotto rice
2 tbsp white wine
1 tbsp lemon juice
3½ cups simmering vegetable stock
finely grated rind of ½ lemon
salt and pepper
1 tbsp chopped fresh parsley
1 tbsp chopped fresh cilantro
sprigs of fresh parsley or cilantro, to garnish

trout fillets with **lime, sesame** & **chili**

SERVES 4 • PREP TIME 10 MINS • COOKING TIME 20 MINS

Heat a nonstick skillet over medium heat, add the sesame seeds, and cook, turning, until they start to color. Tip onto a plate and set aside.

Put the stock into a large skillet and bring to a simmer. Add the trout fillets and poach gently for 7–10 minutes, or until just cooked.

Meanwhile, bring a large pan of water to a boil, add the noodles, and cook for 3 minutes. Drain and toss with the sesame seeds, lime juice, chili, oils, and fish sauce. Keep warm.

To serve, pile an equal quantity of noodles on each of 4 serving plates and top with 2 trout fillets, some watercress, and a lime wedge. Drizzle with a little more sesame oil.

ORGANIC INGREDIENTS

2 tbsp sesame seeds
scant 1¼ cups fish stock
8 trout fillets, about 5½ oz/150 g each
9 oz/250 g dried fine egg noodles
juice of ½ lime
1 fresh red chili, seeded and thinly sliced
1 tbsp sesame oil, plus extra for drizzling
1 tbsp vegetable oil
1 tsp Thai fish sauce
1 bunch watercress
4 lime wedges, to serve

salmon steaks with lime salsa

SERVES 4 • PREP TIME 20 MINS • COOKING TIME 7 MINS + 1 – 2 HRS TO MARINATE

Put the lime rind and juice into a large, shallow, nonmetallic dish that will not react with acid, such as ceramic or glass. Add the garlic and the oil and stir together well. Remove any bones from the fish, rinse the steaks under cold running water, and pat dry with paper towels. Transfer to the dish and coat in the mixture. Cover with plastic wrap and refrigerate for 1–2 hours.

To make the salsa, put the tomatoes in a heatproof bowl and cover with boiling water. Soak for 3–4 minutes, remove from the water, and cool slightly. When cool enough to handle, pierce the skins with the point of a knife. Remove the skins, halve the tomatoes, and remove the seeds. Chop the flesh and put in a bowl. Mix in the remaining salsa ingredients, cover with plastic wrap and refrigerate for 1 hour.

Preheat the broiler to high, cover the broiler rack with foil and brush with oil. Broil the fish for 7 minutes, turning once. Do not overcook. Garnish with mint sprigs and serve with the salsa.

ORGANIC INGREDIENTS

grated rind and juice of 1 lime
1 large garlic clove, crushed
2 tbsp lemon-flavored oil or extra-virgin olive oil, plus extra for brushing
4 organic salmon steaks, about 6 oz/175 g each

LIME SALSA

3 tomatoes
1/3 cup canned lima beans
1 red chili, seeded and finely diced
2 scallions, chopped
juice of 1 lime
1 tbsp chopped fresh mint
1 tbsp chopped fresh parsley
pinch of sugar
salt and pepper

sprigs of fresh mint, to garnish

traditional roast chicken

SERVES 4 • PREP TIME 20 MINS • COOKING TIME 1HR 50 MINS + 10 MINS TO REST

Preheat the oven to 375°F/190°C. In a small bowl, mix 1 tablespoon of the butter with the garlic, walnuts, and parsley. Season well. Loosen the skin from the breast of the chicken without breaking it. Spread the butter mixture evenly between the skin and breast meat. Put the lime quarters inside the body cavity.

Pour the oil into a roasting pan. Transfer the chicken to the pan and dot the skin with the remaining butter. Roast for $1^3/_4$ hours, basting occasionally, until the chicken is tender and the juices run clear when a skewer is inserted into the thickest part of the meat. Lift out and place on a serving platter to rest for 10 minutes.

Blend the cornstarch with the water, then stir into the juices in the pan. Transfer to the stove. Stir over low heat until thickened. Add more water if necessary. Garnish the chicken with lime wedges and rosemary sprigs. Serve with Classic Roast Potatoes, a selection of cooked vegetables, and the thickened juices.

ORGANIC INGREDIENTS

2 tbsp butter, softened
1 garlic clove, finely chopped
3 tbsp finely chopped toasted walnuts
1 tbsp chopped fresh parsley
salt and pepper
1 medium oven-ready chicken, weighing 4 lb/1.8 kg
1 lime, cut into quarters
2 tbsp vegetable oil
1 tbsp cornstarch
2 tbsp water
lime wedges, to garnish
sprigs of fresh rosemary, to garnish
Classic Roast Potatoes (see page 52), to serve
selection of freshly cooked vegetables, to serve

turkey steaks with bean purée

SERVES 4 • PREP TIME 10 MINS • COOKING TIME 25 MINS + 30 MINS TO MARINATE

Wipe the turkey steaks with paper towels and put into a large, shallow dish. Heat the red currant jelly with the vinegar and orange juice in a small pan over low heat and stir until smooth. Pour over the turkey, cover, and let stand for at least 30 minutes.

When ready to cook, heat a stove-top grill pan over high heat until almost smoking. Add the turkey and cook for 5–6 minutes on each side, or until cooked.

Meanwhile, mix all the ingredients for the bean purée together in a bowl, transfer to a nonstick pan over low heat and heat through, stirring frequently, for 6–7 minutes, or until piping hot. Alternatively, transfer the mixture to a microwaveproof container, cover with plastic wrap, and heat in a 1,000-watt microwave oven for 3–4 minutes. Remove and let stand for 2 minutes. Remove and discard the plastic wrap and stir well.

Serve the turkey steaks on the bean purée with freshly cooked green beans, tossed in butter, with cherry tomatoes and scallions, garnished with red currants, if desired.

ORGANIC INGREDIENTS

- 4 turkey breast fillet steaks, about 5 oz/140 g each
- 1 tbsp red currant jelly
- 2 tbsp red wine vinegar
- 1 tbsp orange juice

BEAN PURÉE

- 2 tbsp olive oil
- 1 lb 2 oz/500 g canned cannellini beans, drained, rinsed, and coarsely mashed
- 2–3 garlic cloves, crushed
- 1 tbsp chopped fresh mint

- fresh red currants, to garnish (optional)
- freshly cooked green beans, tossed in butter, with 8 oz/225 g halved cherry tomatoes and 4 chopped scallions, to serve

maple roast lamb with cider

SERVES 4 • PREP TIME 15 MINS • COOKING TIME 3 HRS 15 MINS + 10 MINS TO REST

Preheat the oven to 400°F/200°C. Pour the oil into a roasting pan. Using a sharp knife, trim off and discard any excess fat from the lamb, then make small incisions all over. Transfer the joint to the roasting pan. Put the garlic into a bowl and add the chopped oregano, lemon juice, maple syrup, and salt and pepper to taste. Mix together well. Pour the mixture evenly over the lamb, pushing it into the incisions, then pour over the cider.

Transfer the pan to the preheated oven and roast for 30 minutes, turning once and basting occasionally. Reduce the oven temperature to 300°F/150°C and cook for a further 2¾ hours, or until tender and cooked through. Lift out and place on a serving platter to rest for 10 minutes. Blend the cornstarch with the water, then stir into the juices in the pan. Transfer to the stove. Stir over low heat until thickened. Garnish the lamb with oregano sprigs. Serve with Classic Roast Potatoes, vegetables, and the thickened juices.

ORGANIC INGREDIENTS

2 tbsp lemon-flavored oil or extra-virgin olive oil
5 lb/2.25 kg leg of lamb
1 garlic clove, chopped
1 tbsp chopped fresh oregano
juice of 1 lemon
3 tbsp maple syrup
salt and pepper
3 cups hard cider
1 tbsp cornstarch
2 tbsp water
sprigs of fresh oregano, to garnish
Classic Roast Potatoes (see page 52), to serve
selection of freshly cooked vegetables, to serve

stuffed roast pork with garlic

SERVES 4 • PREP TIME 20 MINS • COOKING TIME 1 HR 45 MINS + 15 MINS TO REST

Preheat the oven to 450°F/230°C. To make the stuffing, melt the butter in a pan over medium heat. Add the garlic and shallots and cook, stirring, for 3 minutes, or until softened. Add the mushrooms and bacon, and cook for another 2 minutes. Remove from the heat and stir in the bread crumbs, sage, lemon juice and rind, and salt and pepper to taste.

Put the stuffing in the middle of the pork loin, then roll up and secure the loin with several lengths of tied string. Place the joint in a roasting pan, then rub the skin with plenty of salt and season with pepper. Brush the honey over the pork.

Cook in the preheated oven for 25 minutes, then reduce the heat to 350°F/180°C. Cook, basting occasionally, for about 1¼ hours, or until cooked through. Remove from the oven and let rest for 15 minutes. Garnish with sage sprigs and serve with Classic Roast Potatoes and vegetables.

ORGANIC INGREDIENTS

2 lb 4 oz/1 kg pork loin, backbone removed and rind scored
2 tbsp honey

STUFFING

6 tbsp butter
1 garlic clove, chopped
2 shallots, chopped
¾ cup chopped mushrooms
4 slices lean bacon, chopped
1¾ cups fresh whole-wheat bread crumbs
1 tbsp finely chopped fresh sage
1 tbsp lemon juice
1 tbsp grated lemon rind
salt and pepper

sprigs of fresh sage, to garnish
Classic Roast Potatoes (see page 52), to serve
selection of freshly cooked vegetables, to serve

steak & vegetable stir-fry

SERVES 4 • PREP TIME 15 MINS • COOKING TIME 5 MINS

Cut the steak across the grain into long, thin strips. Heat the oil in a wok or large skillet over high heat. Add the garlic and scallions and stir-fry for 1 minute. Add the steak and stir-fry for 1 minute.

Add the red and green bell peppers and the cashew nuts, then stir in the lime juice and wine. Season to taste with salt and pepper and stir-fry for another 3 minutes. Scatter over the cilantro. Remove from the heat. Serve with freshly cooked noodles or rice.

ORGANIC INGREDIENTS

1 lb 2 oz/500 g flank or strip steak
2 tbsp vegetable oil
1 garlic clove, chopped
2 scallions, sliced
1 red bell pepper, seeded and sliced
1 green bell pepper, seeded and sliced
3 tbsp unsalted cashew nuts
1 tbsp lime juice
1 tbsp red wine
salt and pepper
1 tbsp chopped fresh cilantro
freshly cooked whole-wheat noodles or brown rice, to serve

desserts

What organic cookbook would be complete without a selection of sumptuous desserts? Within the following pages you will find recipes for every occasion, from juicy Baked Apples in Red Wine, and Fruit Kabobs with Chocolate Sauce, to a satisfying Apple Lattice Tart and a tantalizing Peach & Strawberry Meringue. Chocolate lovers will adore the Chocolate Cups, and what better way to round off a meal than a fragrant Tropical Fruit Salad served with heavy cream? The cakes in this section also make irresistible desserts, or are wonderful served with coffee at any time of day.

baked apples in red wine

SERVES 4 • PREP TIME 15 MINS • COOKING TIME 40 – 45 MINS

Preheat the oven to 400°F/200°C. Using a sharp knife, score a line around the center of each apple. Core the apples, then brush the centers with lemon juice to prevent discoloration. Transfer them to a small roasting pan.

Put the blueberries and raisins into a bowl, then add the nuts, cinnamon, and sugar. Mix together well. Spoon the mixture into the center of each apple, then pour over the wine.

Transfer the stuffed apples to the preheated oven and bake for 40–45 minutes, or until tender. Remove from the oven, then lift out the apples and keep them warm.

Blend the cornstarch with the water, then add the mixture to the cooking juices in the roasting pan. Transfer to the stove and cook over medium heat, stirring, until thickened. Remove from the heat and pour over the apples. Serve with heavy cream.

ORGANIC INGREDIENTS

4 medium cooking apples

1 tbsp lemon juice

½ cup blueberries

½ cup raisins

¼ cup chopped toasted mixed nuts

½ tsp ground cinnamon

2 tbsp soft brown sugar

1 cup red wine

2 tsp cornstarch

4 tsp water

heavy cream, to serve

apple lattice tart

SERVES 4 • PREP TIME 20 MINS • COOKING TIME 50 MINS + 1 HR TO CHILL

To make the pastry, sift the flour and salt into a bowl. Make a well in the center and add the sugar, butter, egg, egg yolk, and water. Mix together to form a smooth dough, adding more water if necessary. Cover with plastic wrap and refrigerate for 1 hour. Preheat the oven to 400°F/200°C. Shape three-quarters of the dough into a ball and roll out on a floured work surface into a circle large enough to line a shallow 10-inch/25-cm tart pan. Moisten and trim the edges. Roll out the remaining pastry and cut into long strips about 1/2-inch/1-cm wide.

To make the filling, spread the jelly over the base of the pastry case, then sprinkle over the nuts. Peel and core the apples, then cut into thin slices. Put them into a bowl with the lemon juice, allspice, golden raisins, grapes, and brown sugar. Mix together gently. Spoon the mixture into the pastry case, then arrange the pastry strips in a lattice over the top. Seal and trim the edges. Bake for 50 minutes until golden. Dust with confectioners' sugar. Serve with ice cream.

ORGANIC INGREDIENTS

PASTRY

2 1/3 cups all-purpose flour, plus extra for dusting
pinch of salt
2 tbsp superfine sugar
1 cup + 2 tbsp butter, diced
1 whole egg plus 1 egg yolk
about 1 tbsp water

FILLING

3 tbsp black currant or plum jelly
1/2 cup chopped toasted mixed nuts
2 lb 2 oz/950 g cooking apples
1 tbsp lemon juice
1 tsp ground allspice
1/2 cup golden raisins
10 grapes, halved and seeded
5 tbsp soft brown sugar

confectioners' sugar, for dusting
ice cream, to serve

fruit kabobs with chocolate sauce

SERVES 4 • PREP TIME 15 MINS • COOKING TIME 15 MINS

Cut the melon flesh into small chunks and put into a bowl. Core the apples and pears, cut into small chunks, and add to the bowl with the lemon juice. Stir together gently. Put the butter into a pan and melt gently over low heat. Stir in the cinnamon and sugar, then remove from the heat and pour into a large, shallow dish. Thread the melon on to skewers, alternating with pieces of apple and pear. When the skewers are full (leave a small space at either end), turn them in the spiced butter mixture until thoroughly coated.

To make the sauce, pour the cream into a small pan and bring gently to a boil over low heat. Remove from the heat, add the chocolate, and stir until melted. Stir in the orange juice and keep warm until required.

Cook the kabobs under a preheated medium broiler, turning frequently, for 10 minutes, or until tender. Remove from the broiler and serve immediately with the warm chocolate sauce.

ORGANIC INGREDIENTS

½ melon, such as honeydew, seeded
2 dessert apples
2 pears
2 tbsp lemon juice
4 tbsp unsalted butter
pinch of ground cinnamon
2 tbsp soft brown sugar

CHOCOLATE SAUCE

½ cup heavy cream
3¼ oz/90 g organic semisweet chocolate, broken into small pieces
2 tbsp orange juice

raspberry ripple ice cream

SERVES 6 • PREP TIME 30 MINS • COOKING TIME 30 MINS +4 HRS TO COOL/FREEZE

Turn the freezer to rapid. Put the raspberries into a pan with the water and bring to a boil, then reduce the heat and let simmer gently for 5 minutes. Remove from the heat and let cool for 30 minutes.

Transfer to a food processor or blender and process to a purée, then rub through a nylon strainer to remove the pips. Set aside.

Beat the eggs in a bowl. Stir the sugar into the warmed milk, then slowly pour onto the eggs, beating constantly. Strain into a clean pan and cook over low heat, stirring constantly, for 8–10 minutes, or until the custard thickens and coats the back of a wooden spoon. Add the vanilla extract, remove from the heat, and let cool.

Half-whip the cream in a large bowl, then slowly stir in the cooled custard. Pour into a freezerproof container and freeze for 1 1/2 hours, or until starting to set around the outside. Remove from the freezer and stir the mixture, breaking up any ice crystals.

Return the mixture to the freezer and freeze for an additional hour, then remove from the freezer and gently stir in the raspberry purée to give a rippled effect. Return to the freezer for an additional hour or until frozen. Serve in scoops with extra fresh raspberries.

ORGANIC INGREDIENTS

1/8 cup fresh or frozen raspberries, thawed if frozen, plus extra to serve
2 tbsp water
2 eggs
1 tbsp superfine sugar
1 1/4 cups milk, warmed
1 tsp vanilla extract
1 1/4 cups heavy cream

carrot cake

MAKES 6 • PREP TIME 20 MINS • COOKING TIME 55 MINS + 40 MINS TO COOL

Preheat the oven to 375°F/190°C. Grease a 7-inch/18-cm square cake pan with butter and line with parchment paper. Sift the flour, salt, allspice, and nutmeg into a bowl. Stir in the brown sugar, then stir in the eggs and oil. Add the carrots, banana, and chopped mixed nuts and mix together well.

Spoon the mixture into the prepared cake pan and level the surface. Transfer to the preheated oven and bake for 55 minutes, or until golden and just firm to the touch. Remove from the oven and let cool. When cool enough to handle, turn out on to a wire rack and let cool completely.

To make the frosting, put the butter, cream cheese, confectioners' sugar, and orange juice and rind into a bowl and beat together until creamy. Spread the frosting over the top of the cold cake, then use a fork to make shallow wavy lines in the frosting. Scatter over the walnuts, cut the cake into bars, and serve.

ORGANIC INGREDIENTS

butter, for greasing

7/8 cup self-rising flour

pinch of salt

1 tsp ground allspice

1/2 tsp ground nutmeg

3/4 cup soft brown sugar

2 eggs, beaten

5 tbsp sunflower oil

3/4 cup (packed) grated carrots

1 banana, chopped

1/4 cup chopped toasted mixed nuts

FROSTING

3 tbsp butter, softened

3 tbsp cream cheese

1 1/2 cups confectioners' sugar, sifted

1 tsp orange juice

grated rind of 1/2 orange

walnut halves or pieces, to decorate

coffee & walnut cake

SERVES 4 • PREP TIME 20 MINS • COOKING TIME 1 HR + 2 HRS 30 MINS TO COOL/CHILL

To make the frosting, put all the ingredients into a food processor and process until creamy. Transfer to a pan and heat, stirring, over a medium heat until bubbling. Cook for 1 minute, then pour into a heatproof bowl. Let cool, then cover with plastic wrap and refrigerate for at least 2 hours.

Preheat the oven to 375°F/190°C. Grease a 9-inch/23-cm loose-bottomed cake pan with butter and line with parchment paper. To make the sponge, sift the flour and baking powder into a bowl, then stir in the sugar. In a separate bowl, beat together the butter, eggs, milk, and coffee, then mix into the flour mixture. Stir in the chopped walnuts and the golden raisins. Spoon the batter into the prepared cake pan and level the surface. Transfer to the preheated oven and bake for 1 hour. Remove from the oven and let cool. When cool enough to handle, turn out on to a wire rack and let cool completely. Spread the frosting over the top of the cold cake, decorate with the walnut halves, and serve.

ORGANIC INGREDIENTS

FROSTING

6 tbsp organic unsweetened cocoa

2 tbsp cornstarch

6 tbsp superfine sugar

½ cup strong black coffee, cooled

1 cup milk

SPONGE

2 cups all-purpose flour

1 tbsp baking powder

7½ tbsp superfine sugar

6 tbsp butter, softened, plus extra for greasing

2 eggs

⅔ cup milk

3 tbsp hot strong black coffee

½ cup chopped walnuts

½ cup golden raisins

walnut halves, to decorate

tropical fruit salad

SERVES 4 • PREP TIME 20 MINS 1 • COOKING TIME 3 MINS + HR TO CHILL

Put the sugar, water, allspice, and lemon rind into a pan. Bring to a boil, stirring continuously, then continue to boil for 1 minute. Remove from the heat and let cool to room temperature. Transfer to a pitcher or bowl, cover with plastic wrap, and chill in the refrigerator for at least 1 hour.

Peel and halve the papaya and remove the seeds. Cut the flesh into small chunks or slices, and put into a large bowl. Cut the mango twice lengthwise, close to the stone. Remove and discard the stone. Peel and cut the flesh into small chunks or slices, and add to the bowl. Cut off the top and bottom of the pineapple and remove the hard skin. Cut the pineapple in half lengthwise, then into quarters, and remove the tough core. Cut the remaining flesh into small pieces and add to the bowl. Add the orange segments and strawberries. Pour over the chilled syrup, cover with plastic wrap, and chill until required. Serve with light or heavy cream, if using.

ORGANIC INGREDIENTS

6 tbsp superfine sugar
1¾ cups water
½ tsp ground allspice
grated rind of ½ lemon
1 papaya
1 mango
1 pineapple
4 oranges, peeled and cut into segments
4½ oz/125 g strawberries, hulled and quartered
light or heavy cream, to serve (optional)

peach & strawberry meringue

SERVES 4 • PREP TIME 30 MINS • COOKING TIME 3 HRS + 1 HOUR TO COOL

Preheat the oven to 225°F/110°C. Line 2 baking sheets with baking parchment, then draw a 10-inch/25-cm circle in the center of each one. To make the meringue circles, in a large bowl, whisk the egg whites into stiff peaks. Whisk in the cream of tartar and salt, then gradually whisk in 1 cup of the sugar. Continue whisking for 2 minutes until glossy. Fill a pastry bag with the meringue mixture and pipe enough to fill each circle. Bake in the preheated oven for 3 hours. Remove from the oven and let cool completely.

In a large bowl, whip the cream with the remaining sugar. Put one meringue circle on to a serving plate, then spread over half the cream. Arrange half the sliced strawberries and peaches on the top, then top with the other meringue circle. Spread over the remaining cream, then top with the remaining fruit. Decorate with mint sprigs and serve.

ORGANIC INGREDIENTS

MERINGUE

- 6 egg whites
- pinch of cream of tartar
- pinch of salt
- 1⅓ cups superfine sugar

FILLING/TOPPING

- 2½ cups heavy cream
- 9 oz/250 g strawberries, hulled and sliced
- 3 ripe peaches, sliced

- sprigs of fresh mint, to decorate

chocolate cups

SERVES 4 • PREP TIME 30 MINS • COOKING TIME 10 MINS + 1 HOUR – 3 HRS 45 MINS TO COOL/FREEZE

Beat together the egg yolks and sugar in a large heatproof bowl until creamy. Heat the milk, vanilla, and cream in a pan over low heat until simmering, then whisk into the egg mixture. Place the bowl over a pan of simmering water. Cook the mixture, stirring, until thick enough to coat the back of a spoon. Stir in the grated lime rind and let cool. Cover with plastic wrap and refrigerate for 1 hour. Transfer to an ice-cream maker and process for 15 minutes. If you do not have an ice-cream maker, use the following freezer method. Put the mixture into a freezerproof container. Cover and freeze for 1 hour, then transfer to a bowl. Whisk to break up the ice crystals then return to the container and freeze for 30 minutes. Repeat twice more, freezing for 30 minutes and whisking each time.

Invert a muffin tray and cover 4 mounds with plastic wrap. Spread the melted chocolate over the mounds. Chill until set. Gently remove the plastic wrap. Serve the ice cream in the cups, sprinkled with lime zest.

ORGANIC INGREDIENTS

6 egg yolks

3/4 cup + 1 tbsp superfine sugar

2 1/4 cups milk

1 tsp vanilla extract

1 cup heavy cream

1 tbsp grated lime rind

4 1/2 oz/125 g organic semisweet chocolate, melted

thin strips of lime zest, to decorate

INDEX